OCT - - 2019

AZTEC

ANCIENT TIMES

EMPIRE

Lori Dittmer

Creative Education · Creative Paperbacks

Published by Creative Education and Creative Paperbacks
P.O. Box 227, Mankato, Minnesota 56002
Creative Education and Creative Paperbacks are imprints
of The Creative Company
www.thecreativecompany.us

Design and production by Chelsey Luther
Art direction by Rita Marshall
Printed in China

Photographs by Alamy (Glasshouse Images, Lebrecht Music & Arts, Alber-
to Masnovo), Corbis (National Geographic Society), Dreamstime (Keng62fa),
FreeVectorMaps.com, Getty Images (Brown Bear/Windmill Books/UIG,
Dorling Kindersley), iStockphoto (pchoui), Shutterstock (koya979)

Library of Congress Cataloging-in-Publication Data
Names: Dittmer, Lori, author.
Title: Aztec Empire / Lori Dittmer.
Series: Ancient times.
Includes index.
Summary: This cultural overview of the Aztec Empire situates the reader
within the society, describing key aspects of daily life, beliefs, and architec-
tural accomplishments such as the Templo Mayor.
Identifiers: LCCN 2018053203 / ISBN 978-1-64026-111-2 (hardcover) /
ISBN 978-1-62832-674-1 (pbk) / ISBN 978-1-64000-229-6 (eBook)
Subjects: LCSH: Aztecs—History—Juvenile literature. / Aztecs—Social life
and customs—Juvenile literature.
Classification: LCC F1219.73.D58 2019 / DDC 972—dc23

First Edition HC 9 8 7 6 5 4 3 2 1
First Edition PBK 9 8 7 6 5 4 3 2 1

CONTENTS

09 Daily Life

20 Aztec Empire Timeline

15 Gods and Sacrifice

22 Glossary

17 The End of the Empire

23 Read More, Websites

05 Step into the Aztec Empire

18 Inside the ... Templo Mayor

24 Index

NORTH AMERICA

AZTEC EMPIRE

Step into the Aztec Empire

Imagine you live in Tenochtitlán. It is the largest **city-state** in the Aztec Empire. Your clothing is made of colorful cotton. This means you are from a **noble** family. Like all children here, you are well behaved. Your people have many rules.

In 1325, people settled on an island
in Lake Texcoco. The site became
the capital city.

By the 1500s, more than 5 million people
made up the Aztec Empire.

Daily Life

Each city-state had a ruler. The head of Tenochtitlán was the emperor. Everyone paid **tribute** to him. When an emperor died, a group of nobles chose a new one.

Nobles lived in brick or stone homes. They took daily steam baths. They ate vegetables and meat. Slaves did most of their work.

CLASSES OF AZTEC SOCIETY

KING
TLATOANI

NOBLES
PIPILTIN

COMMONERS
MACEHUALTIN

SERFS

SLAVES
TLACOTIN

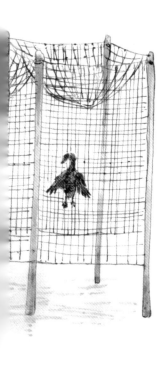

All children went to school. Boys from noble families became priests, warriors, or government leaders. Girls learned to weave cloth and run a household.

Most people in the empire were commoners. Some were **artisans**. Others farmed crops such as beans, peppers, and corn. They kept bees for honey, too. Commoners traded goods at the market.

Gods and Sacrifice

The Aztecs worshiped many gods. Tlaloc was the rain god. The god of the sun and war was Huitzilopochtli. The people used a calendar to keep track of rituals.

The Aztecs believed the gods wanted **human sacrifices**. After a battle, the Aztecs sacrificed their captives. People who broke the rules might be sacrificed, too.

The End of the Empire

Spanish explorer Hernán Cortés arrived in 1519. He eventually destroyed Tenochtitlán with help from other tribes. Cortés built Mexico City over the ruins.

INSIDE THE ...

Templo Mayor

Templo Mayor was the largest Aztec temple. It was finished in 1487. Two **shrines** were at the top. They were for Tlaloc and Huitzilopochtli. The temple was rediscovered in 1978. Today, people can visit the site and a museum about it.

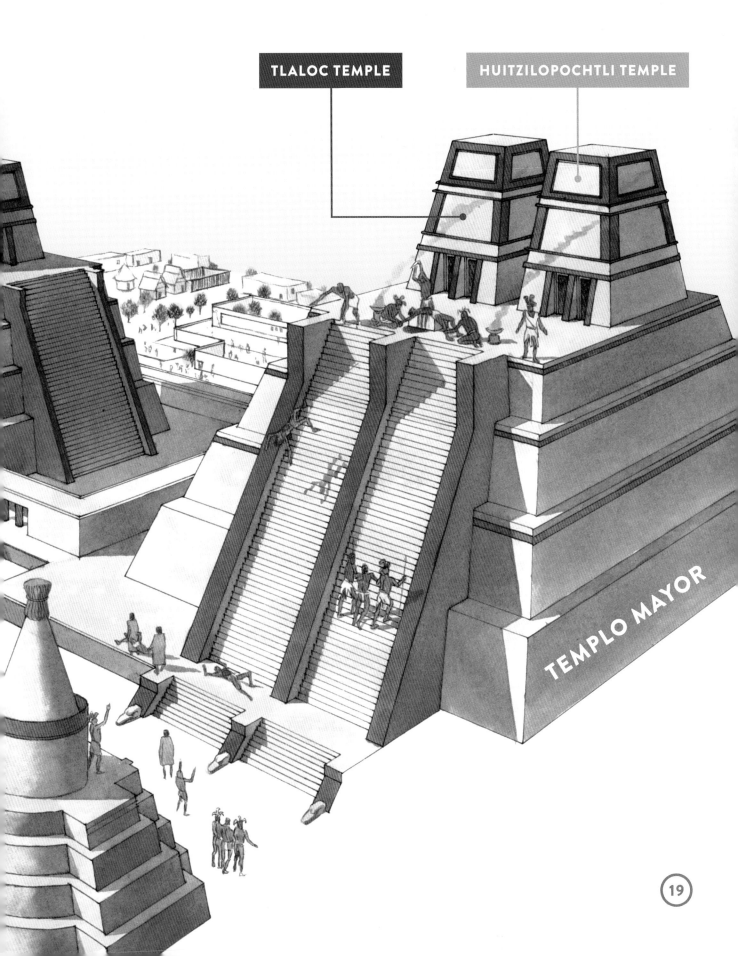

TLALOC TEMPLE

HUITZILOPOCHTLI TEMPLE

TEMPLO MAYOR

19

AZTEC EMPIRE
TIMELINE

1486

As emperor, Ahuitzotl more than doubles the reach of the empire.

1452

A flood leaves Tenochtitlán in ruins.

1487

The seventh and final building phase is complete on the Templo Mayor.

1200s
The Mexica come to central Mexico.

1325
Tenochtitlán is founded.

1440
Moctezuma I becomes the second Aztec emperor.

1428
The "Triple Alliance" of three city-states begins the Aztec Empire.

1502
Moctezuma II becomes emperor.

1521
Spanish explorers destroy Tenochtitlán.

Glossary

artisans: workers who make products by hand

city-state: an independent state that is made up of a city and the surrounding area

human sacrifices: people who are killed on an altar and offered to a god to please the god

noble: of a higher class

shrines: places of religious worship or remembrance

tribute: payment from one state or ruler to another as a sign of dependence

Read More

DeMocker, Michael. *The Aztecs*. Kennett Square, Penn.: Purple Toad, 2015.

Macdonald, Fiona. *You Wouldn't Want to Be an Aztec Sacrifice!* New York: Franklin Watts, 2014.

Niver, Heather Moore. *Ancient Aztec Daily Life*. New York: PowerKids Press, 2017.

Websites

DK Find Out! Aztecs

https://www.dkfindout.com/us/history/aztecs/

Learn more about the Aztec Empire, including what the people ate and the ball game they played.

The School Run: The Aztecs

https://www.theschoolrun.com/homework-help/the-aztecs

Read more about Aztec history and watch a video about the fall of the empire.

Index

calendars 15

city-states 5, 9, 21

clothing 5, 11

commoners 13

Cortés, Hernán 17

education 11

gods 15, 18

human sacrifices 15

Lake Texcoco 6

Mexico City 17

nobles 5, 9, 10, 11

rulers 9, 20, 21

slaves 10

Templo Mayor 18, 20

Tenochtitlán 5, 9, 17, 20, 21

tributes 9